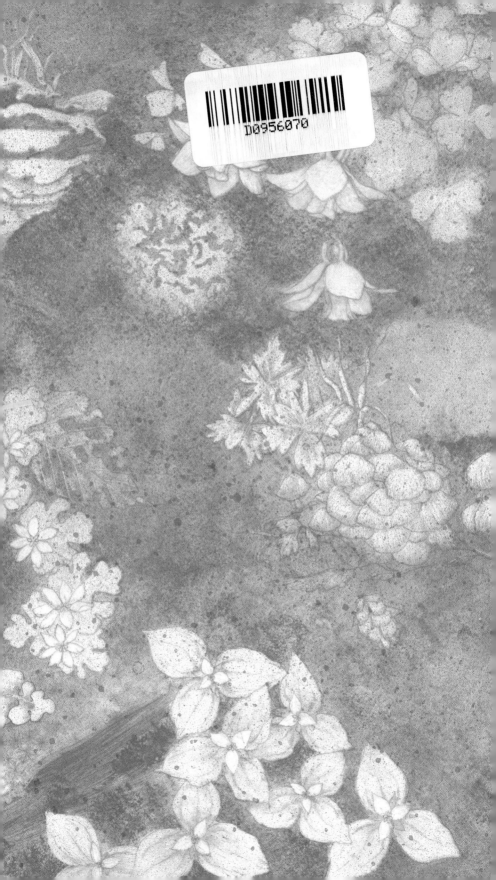

....And Spring Shall Come

By Dean Walley

Illustrated by Tracy McVay

♛ Hallmark Crown Editions

*Snow sculptures the rough contours
of the land in cold perfection....*

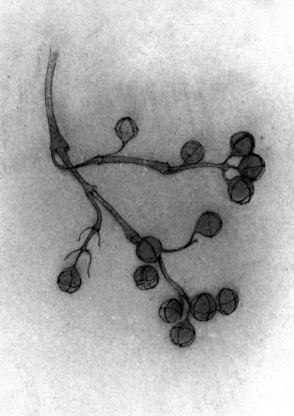

....and spikes of ice,

like frozen tears,

cling to stark black branches....

....as the earth sleeps

through the white silence

of winter.

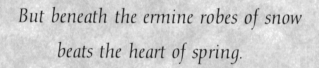

But beneath the ermine robes of snow
beats the heart of spring.

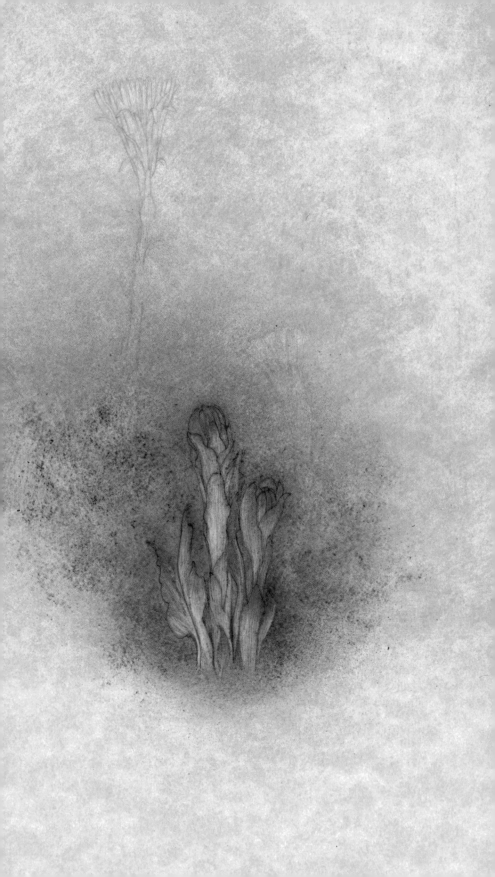

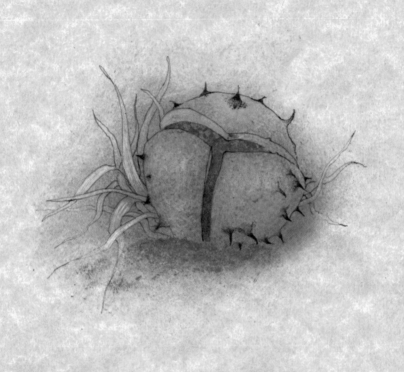

For there are sleeping seeds
dreaming below the drifts....
....filled with life....
....waiting for the warm winds
and the strong sun.

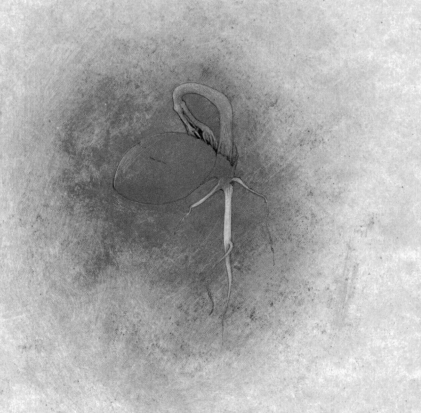

Little packets of life cling

        to the barren branches

              of trees.

And all the animals
are content in their hiding places....
....knowing that spring shall come.

And so it is, in our own hearts....

....when we are lost in a winter

of discontent

or loneliness or sorrow....

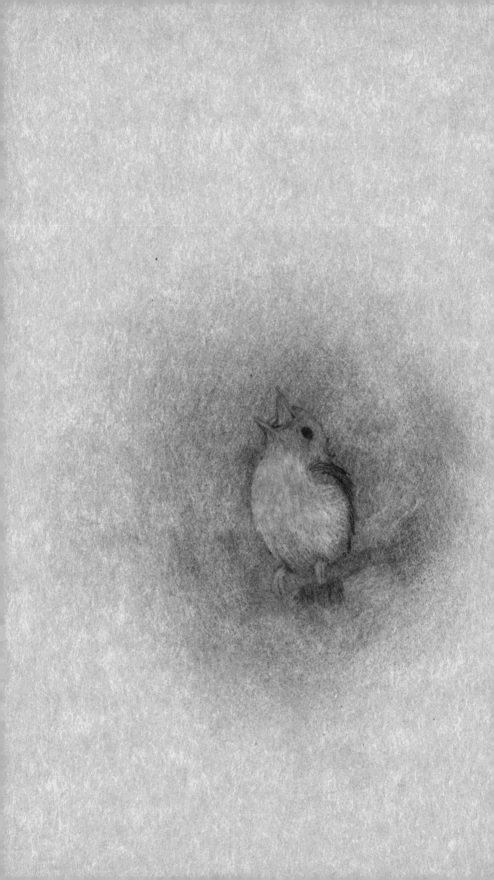

....our spring shall come.

....and faith lives on within us,
strong and unyielding....

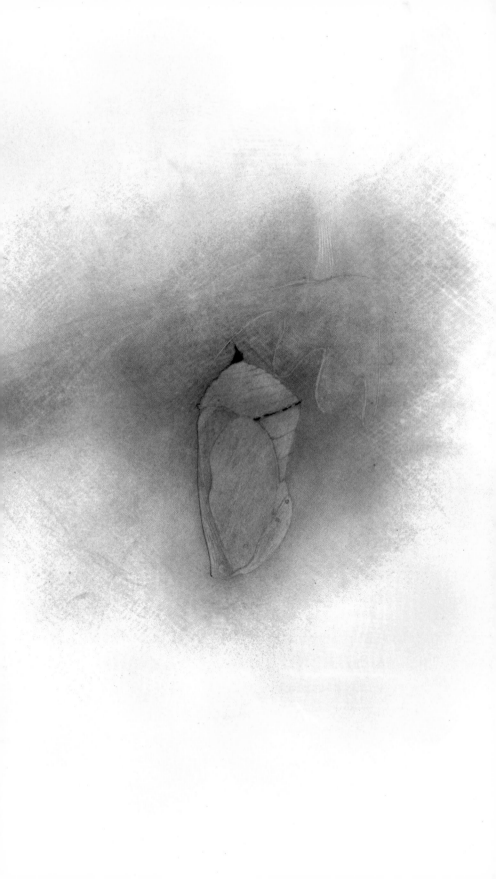

....waiting for the moment
of glad renewal....

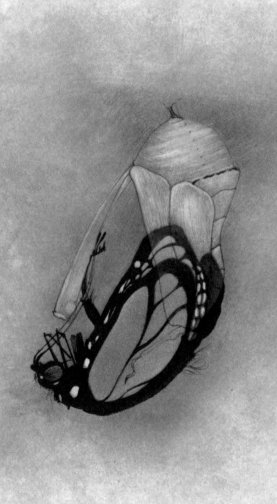

........*when our spring shall come*

....*to bring us joy!*

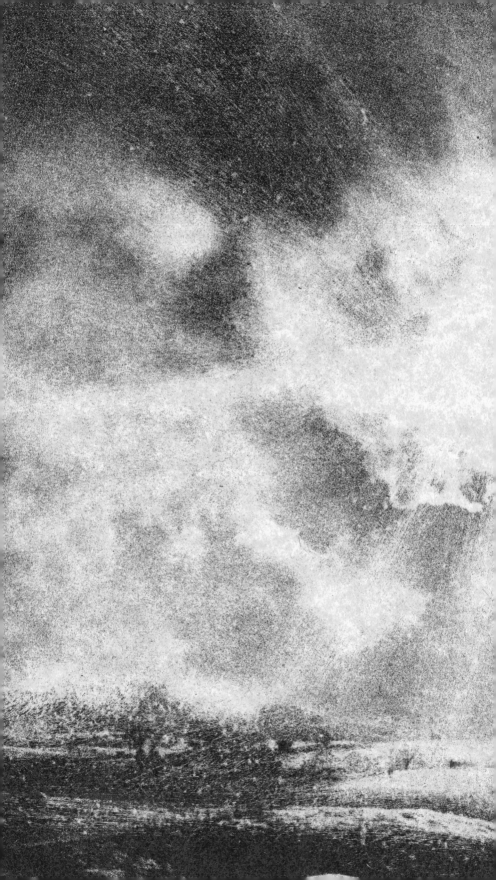

When the season of life and light

blows gently over the winter world....

....and smiles shyly in the gleam

of every sunbeam....

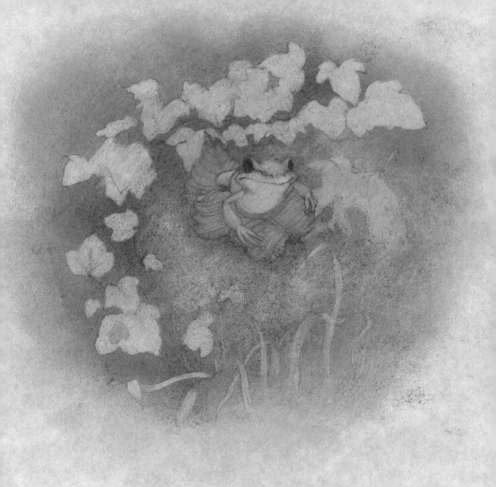

....all of nature

responds to spring's whispered hellos....

....saucy jonquils

pop up through the melting snow....

....jack-in-the-pulpits

dot

the forest floor,

proclaiming the advent

of spring....

....and sparkling brooks

rush down the valleys....

....eager to tell the world

that spring has come at last!

Our spring shall also come....

slowly, but with the certainty
of sunrise....
to every winter-weary heart.

It begins with a touch....a smile....

....a warm word of understanding....

....and the seeds of hope

grow

out of the darkness of our lives....

........and reach for the sun.

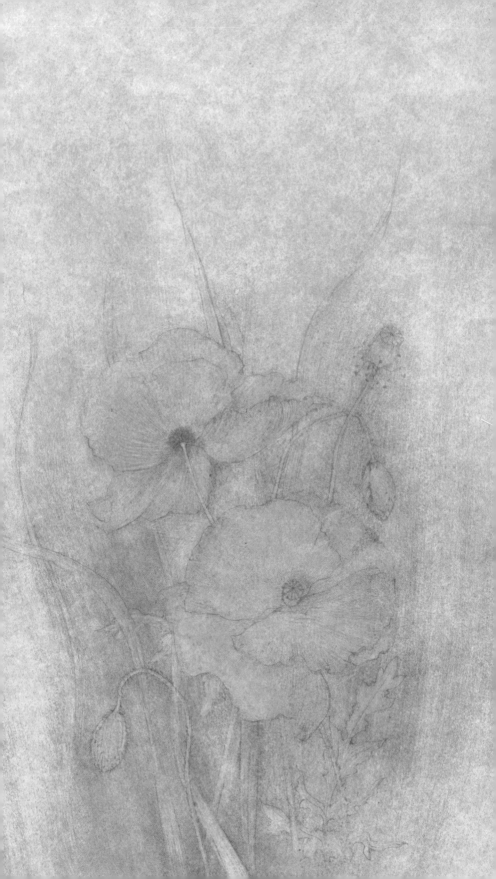

Our faith is full and beautiful
once more....

    ....as perfect as a flower.
And the joy within us streams out....

    ....as vibrant....

      ....and harmonious....
as the colorful patterns woven
by butterflies

    and wildflowers.

Spring is the time of wonder and rebirth

....the first day

of the world....

when the very air is heavy

with fragrance.

The sun fills up the day

and spills

over

into the evening....

....and at night even the ancient stars

seem new.

It is the time of love

and laughter....

....golden with happiness....

....the first day

of the rest of our lives.

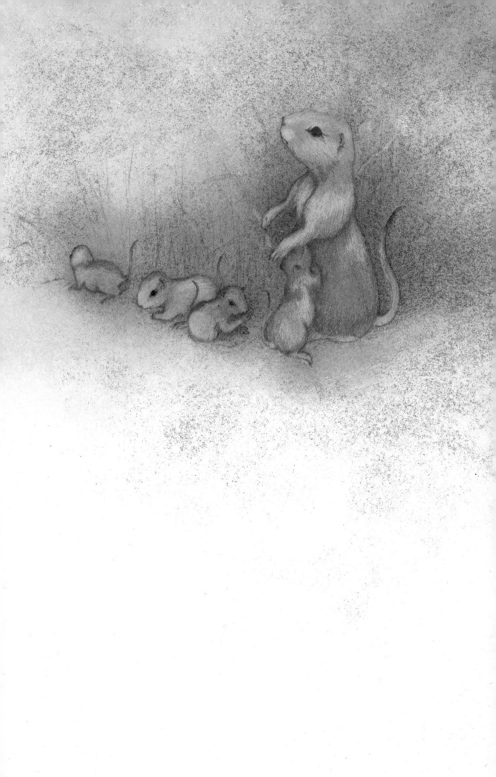

For after winter, spring shall come....

....and the mysterious force

....that touches the seed

....the leaf

....the opening petals....

....touches our hearts, as well.

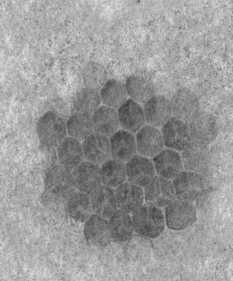

This book was designed and illustrated by Tracy McVay.
The artist made her own color separations and closely
supervised the printing for utmost accuracy of reproduction.
The type is set in a modification of Diotima
Italic, a light typeface originally designed in 1954
by Gudrun Zapf von Hesse for the Stempel Foundry. The
paper is Hallclear, White Imitation Parchment and Ivory
Fiesta Parchment. The cover is bound with natural weave
book cloth and Torino paper.